Know-It-All Library

Military Uniforms

by Jacob Kobelt

The Know-It-All Library
ROURKE ENTERPRISES, INC.
Windermere, Florida 32786

Contents

Published by Rourke Enterprises, Inc., PO Box 929, Windermere, FL 32786. Copyright © 1982 by Rourke Enterprises, Inc., All copyrights reserved. No part of this book may be reproduced in any form without written permission from the publisher. Printed in the United States of America.

Library of Congress Cataloging in Publication Data

Kobelt, Jacob.
  Military uniforms.

  (Know-it-all library)
  Summary: Illustrations and text describe the military uniforms, medals, and decorations of many countries.
  1. Uniforms, Military—Juvenile literature. [1. Uniforms, Military] I. Title. II. Series.
  UC480.K63   335.1'4   82-3659
  ISBN 0-86592-706-5 (lib. bdg.)   AACR2

COVER The West Point cadet on the left is a Plebe, or freshman. The officer on the right wears the insignia of a Distinguished Cadet, a lieutenant, and a First Classman. His uniform is also described on page 17.

How Uniforms Came About

The first uniforms were nothing more than bolts of cloth wrapped around a soldier's waist, or designs emblazoned on rough, everyday workwear. In the heat of battle, these decorations helped distinguish friend from foe. The 1600's brought the Thirty Years War in Europe and large, standing armies. Commanders were expected to outfit and *clothe* their troops. They found it easiest to buy huge quantities of tunics, belts, breeches, caps, and other accessories. For the first time, thousands of soldiers found themselves wearing similar costumes. Decorations sprang up — for generals and drummer boys, for artillerymen and foot soldiers. And whole regiments adopted their own accessories and decorations — sashes, ribbons, stripes, helmets, boots, and more. These have become part of the tradition of armies around the world. Today's ceremonial uniforms are often descended from costumes that are two, three, and even four hundred years old.

The Netherlands

This policeman's furry, sealskin hat is too hot to wear in the summer, but it's part of a tradition that goes back to 1814. That is when the Royal Dutch Gendarmerie was founded. The full-dress uniform seen here includes a double-breasted tunic and short sword. White stripes on the sleeve show the policeman's rank. As he salutes, this man may be thinking of his great, great-grandfather—who could have served in the same unit.

Canada

Bushwhackers and hostile Indians made the Canadian wilderness a dangerous place 100 years ago. In 1873, the Northwest Mounted Police, or Mounties, were formed. These policemen brought law and order to the frontier. They carried the long war lance to impress the Indians. And their brilliant red tunics struck fear into the heart of more than one desperado. Only a few Mounties still ride horses. Motorcycles, cars, and airplanes have replaced most of their mounts.

India

Indian soldiers are proud of their gaily-colored *lungis*, or turbans. Each regiment has its own way of tying the turban, and its own special cloth pattern and decorations. These soldiers are members of the Rajastan Infantry. The unit was formed in the days when India was a British colony. They guarded local rulers and the country's northern frontiers. The tunic is British in style. But these soldiers have added the traditional *cummerbund*, or sash, around the waist.

Portugal

This policeman guards the Portuguese president with watchful eyes. It is part of his duties as a member of the Guardia Nacional Republicana. He wears a Prussian-style helmet, with a pointy metal spike on top. The guard's belt and gloves match his white *gaiters*. They strap under the instep of his boots and button up the side of the leg. Gaiters are an old military fashion. They go back to the days when soldiers wore knee-length breeches!

Italy

Corazzieri guards protect the Italian president. This soldier's plumed helmet makes him look like an ancient Roman centurion. He wears the half-dress uniform for duty at the Presidential Residence. Two plaited cords cross his chest. They are called *aiguillettes*, and were once used to fasten on armor. Today, they show that the soldier is a *gendarme*, a sort of military-policeman. The saber is mainly a symbol of tradition. But if you were to draw it from its scabbard, it would shine brightly!

Australia

The floppy-looking bush hat is an Australian trademark. It dates from the 19th century. In hot climates, a soldier could faint without its protection. This infantry sergeant wears matching white belt and British-style leggings. They make the uniform look smarter on the parade ground. The basic color of the uniform is called *khaki*. In the field, the soldier's khakis help him become invisible. The red sash, of course, is not for camouflage. It's only worn on special ceremonial occasions.

Soviet Union

This Honor Guard wears the tunic and riding breeches of a bygone era. That's because his uniform is for pomp and ceremony, not battle. The Honor Guard Company is made up of men from the Soviet Army, Navy, and Air Force. They are expert at complicated military drills and marches. Notice the patches of color on the soldier's shoulders? Since the time of the Czars, Russian guard units have worn red shoulder straps.

Guatemala

Not one, but seven different uniforms make up this cadet's wardrobe. He is a student at Polytechnic, the military school at Guatemala City. Here, the cadet is outfitted for riding. The puffy riding breeches let his legs bend and flex in the saddle.

Pakistan

The Punjab is known for its tigers, wrestlers, and soldiers. This infantryman belongs to the famous Punjab Regiment. On special occasions, he dons the loose-fitting, fiery-red tunic. It looks like the *kurthas*, or long tunics, worn by ancient Punjab warriors and princes. The special plaid and plumed turban is worn only by members of the regiment. And, the regimental badge is embroidered on the black waist sash.

MEDAL OF HONOR
(United States)

Medals for Courage and Service

PURPLE HEART
(United States)

LEGION OF HONOR
(France)

SILVER STAR
(United States)

**CANADA
SERVICE MEDAL**
(Canada)

Many countries give military decorations, or medals, to soldiers of exceptional merit. This is part of a tradition that goes back to the Middle Ages. The United States awards a medal called the Silver Star for bravery on the battlefield, and its highest award is the Congressional Medal of Honor. Since the Civil War, servicemen have received it for risk of life "above and beyond the call of duty." Great Britain's most important decoration is called the Victoria Cross. It dates from 1856. At the center of the medallion are emblazoned the words, "For Valour." French medals became popular around the time of Napoleon. One such decoration is the Legion of Honor.

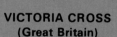

VICTORIA CROSS
(Great Britain)

13

Great Britain

With pride, the Gordon Highlander wears the costume of his forefathers. The huge, plumed headdress makes him look like a furry-headed giant. This Scotsman wears a short jacket called a *coatee*. It is specially designed to be worn with the kilt, or skirt. The sash girding his waist is one worn only by drummers. And the short, broad sword is an old Highlander favorite.

This cavalryman uses his feet to coax along his mount. In this way, his hands are left free to beat a rhythm on the giant kettledrums at his sides. This drummer belongs to the Household Cavalry, the Queen's personal soldiery. The giant drums boom and roar as loudly today as they did in 1805. That is when King George II presented them to these horse soldiers.

United States

Modern uniforms are a great deal simpler than the bedazzling costumes of yesterday. This one (left) dates from 1955. It is the summer dress uniform of a cadet at the United States Air Force Academy. The school trains airmen and other Air Force professionals. It is located near Colorado Springs, Colorado, in the Rocky Mountains. Its 2,500 cadets are divided up into 24 military groups, called squadrons.

This West Pointer (right, page 17) could masquerade as a soldier of President Andrew Jackson's time. Since 1815, the West Point uniform has changed very little. On special occasions, the cadets still wear the green-plumed *shako* hat. It carries the Academy's coat of arms above the visor. By tradition, almost all of the cadets' uniforms are gray, with a little black or white. To graduate from West Point, cadets put in four years of hard study. Then, they serve at least five years in the Army.

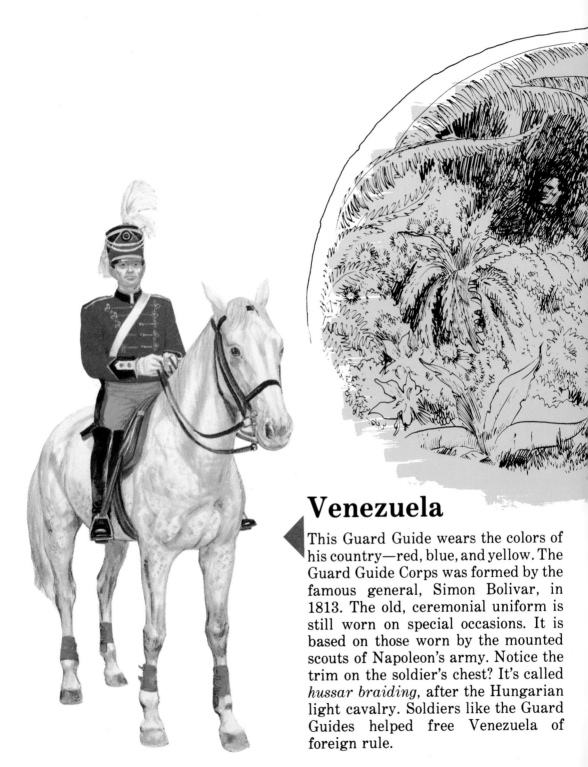

Venezuela

This Guard Guide wears the colors of his country—red, blue, and yellow. The Guard Guide Corps was formed by the famous general, Simon Bolivar, in 1813. The old, ceremonial uniform is still worn on special occasions. It is based on those worn by the mounted scouts of Napoleon's army. Notice the trim on the soldier's chest? It's called *hussar braiding*, after the Hungarian light cavalry. Soldiers like the Guard Guides helped free Venezuela of foreign rule.

Nigeria

In World War II, paratroopers and commandos wore the beret as a sign of valor. This Nigerian sergeant wears it as a member of the United Nations forces. It is his job to keep the peace in troubled parts of the world. The tiny plume is a symbol of the soldier's regiment. Following British army custom, he wears a sash over his shoulder for parades. The color of the sergeant's uniform is called *jungle green*. In the newer African armies, it is fast replacing the old-style khakis.

Greece

Thirty yards of cloth go into the skirt of this Evzone Guard. Greek mountaineers have worn these skirts for centuries. They make it easier to scramble over rocks. Evzones guard the palaces at Athens and Corfu, and the Tomb of the Unknown Warrior. The unit was formed by a Greek king, George I.

Denmark

This Royal Life Guard is a walking museum of military fashion. His unit is one of the oldest in Europe, dating from 1658. The furry, bearskin cap is a momento of the Napoleonic Wars. It was first worn in 1803. The white leather cross belts go back even further — to 1788. The Guards began to wear swords in 1854. They were booty from the First Schleswig War. In 1855, the Guards went back to the original, red-colored tunic. It is now worn on special occasions. The latest addition came in 1955 — white rifle slings for guard duty.

Argentina

This cadet wears a sword with his summer, off-duty uniform. He is a student at the Military Academy of the Argentine. And the sword is of a type worn by a famous countryman, General San Martin. Braided shoulder straps decorate the shoulders of the cadet's white tunic. Long ago, they were used to keep belts and sashes in place. Today, they often carry initials, titles, or regimental badges. Blue trousers with red stripes complete this cadet's uniform.

France

This policeman wears a uniform that has hardly changed in eighty years. His hat, with a fluffy, red pompon, is called a *kepi*. French soldiers have been wearing them since 1884. This guardsman protects the home of the French president. He belongs to the Foot Regiment of the Republican Guard, part of the Gendarmerie Nationale.

The *cuirassier* helmet came into fashion during the Napoleonic Wars. Members of the Republican Guard, Cavalry Section, still wear them. The helmet carries a brass plate bearing the coat of arms of Paris. The Republican Guards wear the same uniform for motorcycle-escort duty. But they remove their saber and cuirassier, and don the modern crash helmet.

Military Academies

West Point

Nations all over the world train their soldiers at special schools, called military academies. The idea of the academy dates back to 1617. That is when a Dutchman named John of Nassau opened the first military academy. Warfare, he decided, was getting to be a more and more complicated business. Successful armies needed a host of expert soldiers. Experts such as artillerymen to accurately bombard enemy armies; engineers to build bridges, roads, and buildings; and mapmakers to survey and draw up charts. The academies taught young soldiers these things. By the early 1800's, the idea had caught on. America's military academy opened at West Point. Almost all of our most famous generals have been educated there. In 1802, the British opened their Royal Military College at Sandhurst. Prussia established the Kriegsakademie, or War Academy. It helped make Prussia one of the most important military powers in Europe. Other famous academies include France's Saint-Cyr, the Royal Military College of Canada, and the Russian Frunze Academy.

Jeffersonville Township Public

Library

P.O. Box 1548

Jeffersonville, IN 47131

DEMCO